The Role of Social Media in the Battle Against Climate Change

Table of Contents

1. Introduction 2

2. Social Media: The Digital Revolution and Its Impact 3

   2.1. The Advent of Social Media 3

   2.2. The Transformative Impact on Communication 3

   2.3. Social Media as a Global Megaphone 4

   2.4. A tool for Socio-Political Changes 5

   2.5. Charting the Path: From Social to Environmental Impact 5

3. Understanding Climate Change: A Concise Overview 7

   3.1. The Science Behind Climate Change 7

   3.2. Observable Effects of Climate Change 8

   3.3. Implications for Human Life and Survival 9

   3.4. Conclusion: A Call to Action 9

4. The Intersection of Social Media and Environmental Activism . . . 11

   4.1. The Rise of a New Medium: Social Media and its Role in
Environmental Activism 11

   4.2. The Digital Generation's Approach to Environmental
Activism 12

   4.3. Amplifying Voices: How Social Media Propels Activism 12

   4.4. Mechanisms of Social Media Activism 13

   4.5. Activism vs. Slacktivism 13

   4.6. Conclusion 14

5. Online Activism: Catalyst for Real World Changes 15

   5.1. The Power of Online Activism 15

   5.2. Social Media Platforms as Stages for Online Activism 15

   5.3. Case Studies Highlighting Successful Online Activism 16

   5.4. Transitioning from Clicktivism to Activism 17

   5.5. Conclusion: The Road Ahead for Online Activism 17

6. Case Studies: Effective Climate Change Campaigns on Social

Media 18

6.1. The Power of Viral Content: The Ice Bucket Challenge 18

6.2. The Proliferation of #FridaysForFuture 19

6.3. Harnessing Memetics: Extinction Rebellion 19

6.4. The Plastic Challenge: #BeatPlasticPollution 20

6.5. Conclusion 20

7. A Deep Dive into #ClimateChange: The Power of Hashtags 22

7.1. Unearthing the Origins: The Birth of Hashtags 22

7.2. #ClimateChange: More Than a Trending Topic 23

7.3. Harnessing the Power of #ClimateChange 23

7.4. Case Studies: Impactful Climate Movements Fueled by
Hashtags 24

7.5. The Multiplicative Effect: Virality and Advocacy 24

7.6. Potential Pitfalls: Surfacing the Dark Side of Hashtags 25

7.7. Moving Forward: Future of #ClimateChange 25

8. Potential Pitfalls: The Challenges of Climate Action on Social
Media 27

8.1. The Muddy Waters of Misinformation 27

8.2. The Inequity of the Digital Divide 28

8.3. The Double-Edged Sword of Slacktivism 28

8.4. An Echo Chamber of Opinions 29

9. Influencers and Celebrities: Amplifying the Green Message 30

9.1. The Relevance of Celebrities and Influencers in Today's
Digital Society 30

9.2. The Effective Use of Celebrity Power for Environmental
Causes 31

9.3. The Role of Influencers in Disseminating the Climate
Change Message 31

9.4. The Potential Pitfalls: False Information and Performative
Activism 32

9.5. Concluding Thoughts: A Call to Responsible Influence 32

10. From Awareness to Action: Implementing Digital Strategies for Change 34

10.1. Harnessing the Power of Social Media 34

10.2. Interactive Communication: A Key Strategy 35

10.3. Spotlights and Stories: The New Digital Storytelling 35

10.4. Taking Actions Beyond Likes and Shares 36

10.5. Usage of Analytics for Measuring Impact 36

11. The Future of Social Media in Climate Change Advocacy 38

11.1. The Burgeoning Role of Social Media 38

11.2. e-Petitions and Crowd Funding: Facilitation of Grassroots Movements 39

11.3. Social Media as an Arena for Climate Change Debates 39

11.4. Influence of Social Media Algorithms on Climate Advocacy. 40

11.5. Integrating AI and Data Analytics: An Emerging Trend 40

11.6. Moving Forward: Uniting Digital Strategies with Real-world Action 41

There's a lot that's at stake here, but if everything's at stake, then everyone has a role to play.

Chapter 1. Introduction

The world is increasingly turning digital and amidst this vast world of tweets, shares, and stories, our planet's health is becoming a trending topic. In our Special Report, "The Role of Social Media in the Battle Against Climate Change," we discern how this modern phenomenon is revolutionizing environmental activism. It's not tech jargon and algorithms, but a story unfolding in the palms of our hands, accessible to everyone. This radiant report will catch your eyes as we demonstrate the compelling ways social media platforms are boosting climate consciousness globally. Brace yourself for an enlightening narrative that not only keeps you informed but motivates you to be a part of this urgent, digital-led crusade. Invest in understanding and join us in this green revolution - one share, one post, one story at a time. Let's change together, since after all, the discussion for a sustainable future is 'trending' right now!

Chapter 2. Social Media: The Digital Revolution and Its Impact

The genesis of the digital age has undeniably walked hand in hand with the rapid proliferation of social media platforms. The extremes of our world now lie at our fingertips, through familiar platforms like Facebook, Twitter, Instagram, LinkedIn, and many more. These esteemed platforms have not only transformed the landscape of interpersonal communication but have also significantly influenced social, cultural, political, and now, environmental facets of contemporary life.

2.1. The Advent of Social Media

The genesis of social media can be traced back to the latter part of the 20th century, with the conceptualization of the internet. From the humble origins of SixDegrees.com to the modern frenzy around platforms like Twitter, Facebook, and Instagram, social media platforms have constantly evolved to become the dominant force in digital interaction. Indeed, as of 2020, the global count of social media users surpassed a staggering 3.6 billion. This figure is projected to grow to nearly 4.41 billion by 2025, emphasizing the influence and reach of this digital revolution.

2.2. The Transformative Impact on Communication

The impact of social media on communication is multifaceted and profound. It has fundamentally transformed various aspects of our lives, including the very nature of human interaction. With just a few clicks or taps, we can now instantly connect and communicate with people across continents, free from the constraints of geographic boundaries. This has fostered a culture of rapid information dissemination, instant feedback, and real-time conversations – interlacing strangers and kindred spirits alike - in an intricate global web of digital communication.

Moreover, social media enables every user to create, share, or exchange information, opinions, and multimedia content, bridging the historical divide between active content creators and passive content consumers. The traditional top-down approach to information distribution has been reinstated with a more democratic and decentralized paradigm. This shift has, in essence, democratized the media landscape.

2.3. Social Media as a Global Megaphone

An important aspect of social media's impact is its function as a 'global megaphone'. News, views, and issues can spread faster and wider than any traditional media could ever allow, reaching millions of users within seconds. Crucial social issues, which were once stifled in a sea of traditional media filters, can now rise to the global stage through the sheer force of shares, likes, retweets, and hashtags.

Moreover, social media's ease of access and pervasiveness have allowed voices from marginalized and underrepresented groups to rise into prominence. Advocacy groups, activists, and non-government organizations leverage this reach to disseminate their message, united by the sole purpose - to effect change.

2.4. A tool for Socio-Political Changes

With its expansive reach and swift communication, social media has become a potent tool for political discourse and social change. It played an instrumental role in movements such as the 'Arab Spring' in North Africa and the Middle East, Ukraine's Euromaidan uprising, and the 'Black Lives Matter' movement in the United States, to name a few.

The power of social media in effecting socio-political change is underpinned by its capacity to mobilize widespread discourse and galvanize collective action. This dynamism of social media's digital community breathes life into grassroots movements, increases transparency, builds participatory democracy, and allows for reckoning against various social ills.

2.5. Charting the Path: From Social to Environmental Impact

The purview of social media's impact on society is not limited to socio-political narratives but also extends to environmental arenas. An increasing number of eco-conscious individuals, influencers, advocacy groups, and organizations are leveraging social media to catalyze discussion and action on environmental issues, most prominently, climate change.

The discourse around climate change has truly taken on a global character in the digital space. The #ClimateChange hashtag has become a rallying cry for environmental advocates worldwide, spawning a plethora of sub-movements and discussions, including #FridaysForFuture, #ClimateStrike, #ClimateAction, and more.

The potential of social media as a tool for environmental activism is immense and growing. While it is not without its share of challenges, it is certainly breathing fresh air into the climate change discourse, by building awareness, fostering engagement, inciting action, and creating a global community united by the cause of saving our planet.

In conclusion, social media's revolutionary impact on the digital world can be succinctly summarized as one that empowers, connects, and influences. As we continue to traverse through the complexities of the environmental crisis, the power of this digital revolution could very well be the deciding factor in tipping the balance in favor of our planet. The next chapters will delve into greater detail, discussing and dissecting the intersection of social media and environmental activism, the workings of online activism, and the role of influencers and celebrities in amplifying the green message, among other pertinent topics.

Chapter 3. Understanding Climate Change: A Concise Overview

Climate change, a quintessentially global concern, has formed the bedrock of countless discussions, debates, and deliberations in recent years. The health of our planet hangs in the balance, subjected to an onslaught of alterations ostensibly wrought by human actions. Understanding climate change, therefore, becomes a critical foundation for any nonchalant observer or fervent advocate for environmental preservation and regeneration.

3.1. The Science Behind Climate Change

Let's establish this: Climate change refers unequivocally to long-term shifts in temperatures and weather patterns. The distinction between climate change and weather events, which are typically short-term, is paramount. Climate change encompasses not just rising average temperatures, but a complex mix of shifting weather patterns, increasing sixe of desert areas, melting ice caps, and more.

The root of climate change can be traced back to the greenhouse effect, a natural process which maintains our planet's habitable temperature. This phenomenon involves gases in the earth's atmosphere, nicknamed 'greenhouse gases', which include predominantly Carbon Dioxide (CO_2), but also Methane (CH_4), Nitrous Oxide (N_2O), and others. These gases trap some of the sun's heat, preventing it from escaping back into space, much like the glass walls of a greenhouse.

However, the trouble begins when this balance encounters a

disturbance. Human activities, specifically burning fossil fuels and deforestation, are leading to an excessive buildup of greenhouse gases, particularly CO2, in the atmosphere. This surplus hampers the natural atmospheric balance, locking more heat on our planet, thereby, leading to an overall warming effect – global warming, which in turn drives climate change.

3.2. Observable Effects of Climate Change

Now that we've compressed the crux of the science behind climate change let's delve into its tangible manifestations. The effects of climate change stretch beyond the proverbial 'rising temperatures' and seep into almost every facet of Earth's ecosystem, upending life as we know it.

The most staggering indication of climatic shifts is undoubtedly the rise of global average temperature, marking a consistent upward spiral since the late 19th century. This has led to more frequent and intense heat waves, disrupting wildlife and human life alike.

Discoloration and melting of polar ice caps and glaciers, known as glacier retreat, pose another stark evidence of climate change as the increased warmth slowly erodes these icy landscapes. This ties directly to another alarming effect – the rise in sea levels. Thermal expansion and added water from melting ice culminate in coastlines disappearing, threatening low-lying islands and coastal cities.

A growing litany of changes also highlights shifting precipitation patterns leading to increased droughts and wildfires, heavy rainfall, and even more potent storms. Its ripple effect is indeed a threat to biodiversity as lack of water or too much of it affects both flora and fauna. Climate change also touches the oceans; warmer oceans harm marine life and spawn more severe or frequent tropical storms.

3.3. Implications for Human Life and Survival

Having recognized the stark impacts of climate change on the planetary scale, it is also crucial to acknowledge the potential implications for human life and survival.

Climate change, by disrupting ecosystems, spells trouble for the agricultural sector, essentially risking our food security. Altered weather patterns, unpredictable seasons, and extreme weather events could lead to crop failures and livestock deaths. This adversely impacts not just the availability but also the nutritional value of food.

Humans' health could take a hit with the rising heat intensifying the spread of some diseases and creating a new pattern of health emergencies. The increased warmth and widespread precipitation changes will cause geographic redistribution of disease vectors like mosquitoes, expanding the regions vulnerable to vector-borne diseases. Moreover, heat waves can lead to dehydration, heat stroke, and cardiovascular failures, exacerbating health concerns, especially amidst the elderly.

Climate change does not stop at posing health risks and threatening food security; it can, in fact, give rise to climate refugees. As sea-level rises and extreme weather events become more frequent, many could be forced from their homes, leading to a surge in displaced people and potentially even conflict.

3.4. Conclusion: A Call to Action

The discourse around climate change cannot afford to be solely academic. The current trajectory nudges us closer to a 1.5°C-2°C global temperature rise relative to pre-industrial times within this century, recognized by scientists as the threshold that could herald irreversible impacts. We stand on the precipice of time where we must transform how we interact with the planet.

Yet, this battle is not one devoid of hope. Concrete steps by individuals, societies, and governments – a coalition of willing, conscious actors – can still underline a significant difference. Future chapters in this discourse will explore the specific ways in which social media is galvanizing this collective global response to climate change. After all, 'the world at our fingertips' can emerge as 'the world saved by our fingertips'. Let's type, shall we, a story of redemption, resilience, and relentless resolve.

Chapter 4. The Intersection of Social Media and Environmental Activism

At first glance, it might seem strange to contemplate the intersection of social media and environmental activism. However, upon closer inspection, the correlation becomes increasingly apparent. This complex entanglement, a product of our exceedingly digitized era, is transforming the spectrum of awareness, education, and activism surrounding the fight against climate change.

4.1. The Rise of a New Medium: Social Media and its Role in Environmental Activism

Social media platforms - a category which includes the likes of Facebook, Twitter, Instagram, TikTok - have rapidly become a major influencer in people's lives globally. With the touch of a screen or a click of a mouse, news can spread to the four corners of the earth in the span of minutes. Environmental activists have used this potential to their advantage, taking to social media to spread awareness, incite change, and garner support for crucial environmental causes.

As a tool for communication, social media is unparalleled. It is not bound by geography or time zones, and it is accessible to anyone with internet access. This configuration makes social media an incredibly effective platform for sharing information and mobilizing support for environmental initiatives. News articles, videos, research findings, and personal stories all make their way onto the feeds of users globally, fostering a digitally-cultivated consciousness about the state of our planet.

4.2. The Digital Generation's Approach to Environmental Activism

The younger generation, known as Gen Z, has shown a deep concern for the environment, using various social media platforms to voice their worry and drive action. Here, activism takes on many forms - petitions shared and signed in seconds, protest events broadcasted live across the globe, and thought-provoking content liked, shared, and retweeted. This digital-savvy cohort is changing the traditional dynamics of activism by pushing for environmental justice through digital spaces.

Understanding the appeal of different platforms has also been a key strategy for young activists. For instance, Instagram, with its visually appealing interface, is a fantastic avenue for sharing shocking photographs and infographics that communicate the stark reality of climate change. Twitter's succinct format caters brilliantly to timely, brief broadcasts about the latest environmental news, while TikTok, through its short videos often accentuated with wit and humor, successfully reaches a wide and diverse audience.

4.3. Amplifying Voices: How Social Media Propels Activism

One of the most profound features of social media is its ability to amplify voices that are often unheard. Previously, mainstream media had the upper hand, controlling the dissemination of information. However, social media has democratized the scene, offering a platform where activists, experts, and concerned citizens alike can share their perspectives, unfiltered and uncommented upon.

In an environmental context, this means local communities facing deforestation, pollution, and other forms of environmental degradation can share their stories broadly on these platforms, grabbing global attention and rallying support. When these personal narratives go viral, they put pressure on decision-makers and can lead to tangible policy changes.

4.4. Mechanisms of Social Media Activism

While social media's role in amplifying voices and spreading awareness is evident, it's worth diving deeper into how it facilitates activism.

Firstly, let's talk about the power of hashtags. These symbolic markers began as simple metadata tags on Twitter but have now evolved into a potent tool for movement-building and message amplification across all major platforms. Significant climate-related global movements like #FridaysForFuture, #ClimateStrike, and #SaveAmazonia all began with a single hashtag, demonstrating the remarkable ability of social media to connect people across borders, languages, and cultures.

Second, social media platforms also provide prominent features that can be leveraged by activists. For instance, Twitter's retweeting capacity creates an ever-widening network of shares, reaching audiences that were previously unreachable. Similarly, features on TikTok like 'duet' and 'stitch' enable activists to contribute to ongoing conversations, fostering a community of engaged climate enthusiasts.

4.5. Activism vs. Slacktivism

Despite the undeniable impact of social media in advocating for climate action, it also invites the debate on 'activism vs. slacktivism'. Slacktivism refers to the act of showing support for a cause online, such as liking a post or sharing a link, without any meaningful or hands-on involvement. Critics argue that such shallow engagement can create a false sense of activism and deter real-world action.

The border between activism and slacktivism is blurry, and while it's true that sharing a post doesn't equate to actual action, it's important to acknowledge the potential of each share in raising awareness and instigating conversations. With strategic implementation and follow-up actions, the danger of slacktivism can be mitigated, and social media platforms can be effectively utilized as a launchpad for real, meaningful climate action.

4.6. Conclusion

The intersection of social media and environmental activism is ultimately a dynamic one. In its endless stream of data, social media has created an avenue where activism can occur on a scale previously unimaginable. It's thus up to us, users and activists alike, to harness this tool with great responsibility and ensure that the digital revolution propels us towards a more sustainable future. We must remember that in this fight against climate change, every tweet, share, and post could be the one that makes a difference.

Chapter 5. Online Activism: Catalyst for Real World Changes

In this chapter, the all-encompassing nature of social media will be carved masterfully, portraying its potential to be a massive driving force for climate activism. Let's plunge into this digital world and explore how social media activism can catalyze real-world changes.

5.1. The Power of Online Activism

Online activism, also referred to as digital activism, has drastically expanded the sphere of participation, enabling anyone with internet access to voice their opinions, volunteer their time, or donate their money to a worthy cause. In the context of environmental action, online activism is not only about raising awareness. It is about inspiring action, influencing public policy, and persuading corporations to be more sustainable.

The accessibility of digital media platforms presents unparalleled opportunities for activism. As a fundamental democratizing force, they extend the opportunity for involvement to those who cannot physically participate in demonstrations or donate to support climate change initiatives.

5.2. Social Media Platforms as Stages for Online Activism

Social media platforms function as stages on which people can advocate for change. Thanks to social networks, distant voices merge into unified shouts that can facilitate directional change. Platforms such as Facebook, Twitter, Instagram, and LinkedIn now offer more than just a space to connect with others - they have become battlefields for activists fighting for a sustainable future.

On Twitter, activists can tag relevant policymakers, demand action, and pressure governments into taking steps towards more environmentally friendly legislation. Meanwhile, Instagram's visual appeal allows activists to share powerful images and stories about the direct impact of climate change. Facebook's reporting features and LinkedIn's professional networks can amplify the reach of these messages, creating a snowball effect that drives change not only online but in the real world too.

5.3. Case Studies Highlighting Successful Online Activism

There are plentiful examples of successful online activism. The Online Climate Strike, an offshoot of the Greta Thunberg-led Fridays for Future movement, was a global event promoting the protection of the environment. When the Covid-19 pandemic mitigated in-person protests, these activists turned to digital platforms. They posted pictures of their homemade placards, with hashtags such as #climatestrikeonline, reaching millions of people worldwide.

Another remarkable example is the Shell Oil "Arctic Ready" campaign, in which users were invited to create their warning labels for Shell's proposed Arctic oil drilling. The idea was hijacked by Greenpeace activists, who posted satirical and critical labels tagging Shell. The campaign created significant backlash, thus influencing Shell's public image and policy indirectly.

These cases affirm the power of online activism, demonstrating how social networking can amplify voices that propel significant changes in the real world.

5.4. Transitioning from Clicktivism to Activism

The term 'clicktivism' refers to the ecosystem wherein online users 'click' to signify their support for a particular issue. While clicktivism earns criticism for being too easy, fostering surface-level engagement, it has great potential. Online activities like signing online petitions, sharing informative posts, tagging organizations, or funding crowdfunding campaigns can all engender change. The trick is transitioning from clicktivism to activism, from passive sharing to active contribution. And social media platforms are just the platforms to facilitate this transition.

5.5. Conclusion: The Road Ahead for Online Activism

The ongoing digital evolution of activism offers immense prospects for controlling climate change. The convenience of sharing and connecting, selective audience targeting, cost-effectiveness, massive outreach, and most importantly, the potential to influence behaviors and policies, makes online activism an invaluable tool in the fight against climate change.

Nonetheless, like any tool, its efficacy is dependent on how well it is utilized. As we journey ahead, it becomes crucial to navigate the virtual realm strategically, innovatively, and responsibly, communicating climate science accurately, advocating sustainable behaviors, and motivating enactment of eco-friendly policies. The endeavors of today's digital activism carry the profound capacity to make a discernable difference in our shared pursuit for a sustainable future. Let's ensure we wield this powerful digital tool prudently.

Chapter 6. Case Studies: Effective Climate Change Campaigns on Social Media

In examining the dynamic arena of climate change activism, we stumble upon a plethora of campaign examples that have successfully harnessed the power of social media platforms in promoting the verdant cause. These campaigns, through the use of compelling narratives, innovative approaches and strategic execution, have effectively amplified climate consciousness around the globe. So, let's unravel the stories embedded in these online crusades and discern the underpinnings of their success.

6.1. The Power of Viral Content: The Ice Bucket Challenge

In the realm of social media campaigns, the Ice Bucket Challenge stands as a powerful testament to the impact and potency of viral content. While not directly related to climate change, this phenomenally successful campaign nonetheless provides valuable insights. The Challenge saw millions of internet users, celebrities and everyday people alike, drenching themselves with a bucket of ice-cold water, filming it, and then nominating others to do the same. All of this was aimed at raising awareness for the neurodegenerative disease ALS.

The key to the extraordinary success of the Ice Bucket Challenge lies in its highly visual, interactive, and "fun" nature, which seized the interest of social media users across the world. Climate change campaigns can extract a valuable lesson from this: weaving engagement and a sense of communal participation in a fun and visually interesting way can significantly boost a campaign's viral reach and impact.

6.2. The Proliferation of #FridaysForFuture

One of the most influential and popular social media campaigns for climate change emerged from a humble bench outside the Swedish Parliament. A young girl, Greta Thunberg, began skipping school to protest against the lack of action on the escalating climate and ecological crisis. Her simple sign, 'Skolstrejk för klimatet' (School Strike for the Climate), and the hashtag #FridaysForFuture quickly became the rallying cry for climate activism across the globe.

Greta's youth, determination and eloquent speeches struck a chord with millions worldwide, giving rise to an immense wave of school strikes and protests. The power of this campaign lies primarily in its raw authenticity, the relentless conviction of its torchbearer, and the palpable urgency conveyed by her speeches. Social media platforms served as the vital conduit for her message, allowing it to reach and mobilize a global audience.

6.3. Harnessing Memetics: Extinction Rebellion

Understanding the power of memes and viral content, the Extinction Rebellion movement turned climate activism into a 'cool' and 'hip' orientation. The symbol of the hourglass in a circle became iconic, a simple, potent symbol representing time running out for many species unless drastic action is taken on climate change.

The case of Extinction Rebellion demonstrates the power of symbolic imagery and meme culture in attaining vast reach and virality on social media. The success of this campaign lies in the clever combination of powerful unifying symbols, disruptive peaceful protests, and the omnipresence of social media. This movement, through its innovative approach, has completely reignited the field of climate activism, proving that creative disruptions coupled with potent symbols and consistent messaging can be incredibly effective.

6.4. The Plastic Challenge: #BeatPlasticPollution

Social media became a significant force for environmental activism when the United Nations Environment Program (UNEP) launched the #BeatPlasticPollution campaign. As a part of the campaign, people were encouraged to share photos of themselves replacing single-use plastic items with environmentally friendly alternatives.

Notable public figures and celebrities, such as Arnold Schwarzenegger and Dia Mirza, jumped aboard the viral hashtag. Soon, thousands of people worldwide were making different eco-friendly swaps and sharing their stories on social media. The power of #BeatPlasticPollution lies in its simplicity, personalizing the mission, and the collective responsibility it fostered. Showing an individual's small changes can contribute to the global fight against plastic pollution transformed spectators into active participants.

6.5. Conclusion

As the above case studies demonstrate, successful climate change campaigns on social media share some common attributes. They deliver a simple and strong message, they resonate with a broad audience, and they provide an avenue for people to become involved. However, they also brilliantly leverage the unique features of social media - virality, visibility, interactive, communal participation, and opportunity for personal expression.

As we march towards a future fraught with climatic uncertainties, these digital tools and platforms offer a ray of hope. With strategic, innovative, and inclusive campaigns, social media holds the potential to galvanize global collective action, transforming online outreach into tangible real-world change. The lessons derived from these successful campaigns should guide future digital climate crusades, increasingly raising global climate consciousness and prompting necessary actions.

Remember, the discussions around climate change are not confined to intellectual and expert circles - they are a collective conversation. And social media platforms empower each of us to contribute to this global narrative. So, let's share, let's participate, let's drive action - because every tweet, post or share could spark the flame for a greener, healthier world.

Chapter 7. A Deep Dive into #ClimateChange: The Power of Hashtags

The digital landscape of today has progressed in leaps and bounds, transfiguring the very fabric of human communication. In this broad spectrum of communication platforms, hashtags, a vernacular indigenous to social media ecosystems, have evolved as potent forces. Hashtags are more than just metadata, they're channels for worldwide discourses, rallying cries for collective movements, and, in the context of our subject, fundamental tools for climate activists across the globe.

7.1. Unearthing the Origins: The Birth of Hashtags

The advent of the hashtag can be traced back to 2007, when social media entrepreneur Chris Messina proposed using the pound (#) symbol to group relevant topics on Twitter. It was not long before this suggestion broke barriers and spiraled forth to permeate across multiple social media spaces.

Nowadays, hashtags have evolved into ubiquitous symbols across various social media platforms, serving as linchpins, connecting the scattered discourse in our increasingly digitized world. They wield immense power to guide public sentiments, shape perceptions, and steer conversations towards critical issues such as climate change.

7.2. #ClimateChange: More Than a Trending Topic

It's fascinating to note how climate activism has found solid ground in the precincts of social media, bolstered by the power of hashtags. '#ClimateChange', one of the most popular and influential markers, does not merely denote a trend but powers a worldwide movement.

'#ClimateChange' transcends linguistic borders, geographic constraints, and cultural nuances to unify users in one collective call for action against the perils facing our planet. It is a symbol that underlines common ground and collective solidarity to promote urgency, disseminate credible information, and draw attention to the significance of the cause.

7.3. Harnessing the Power of #ClimateChange

Climate change's enormity and complexity are often overwhelming, making it challenging to be fully informed about every related issue. Hashtags provide a solution as they curate a montage of posts, articles, images, and videos, enabling users to grasp the multifaceted narrative with ease.

Another advantage lies in the simplicity of the hashtag function. Activists, scientists, educators, and influencers can cogently communicate their messages to the public, bypassing traditional information gatekeepers. What's more, the employment of visually appealing media such as images and infographics drives greater user engagement.

7.4. Case Studies: Impactful Climate Movements Fueled by Hashtags

Several trends showcase the powerful influence of hashtags. '#FridaysForFuture', started by teen activist Greta Thunberg, ignited a worldwide movement of weekly school strikes for climate action. The hashtag '#ClimateStrike', borne from this movement, has been a rallying cry for a generation demanding accountability from their leaders.

Similarly, the global campaign '#ClimateAction' expands beyond pressing for policies - it is a call to the masses to make lifestyle changes. '#ZeroWaste' and '#SustainableLiving' are also popular hashtags that amplify efforts towards eco-friendly lifestyles, contributing to the larger cause.

7.5. The Multiplicative Effect: Virality and Advocacy

Hashtags, when they go viral, can generate attention on an exponential level. A shared post here, a retweeted video there - the cumulative effect can result in widespread advocacy.

However, for the sheer scale to transform into real-world impact, it requires strategically constructed messages, visually resonating content, active user engagement, and relevant influencers who can amplify the reach. It's not just about numbers, but a nuanced blend of elements steering virality for positive change.

7.6. Potential Pitfalls: Surfacing the Dark Side of Hashtags

While understanding the power of hashtags, it is equally crucial to recognize their potential pitfalls. The phenomena of 'slacktivism' – a portmanteau of slacker and activism – refers to the downside of digital activism where a simple share or like replaces the commitment to real-world action.

Moreover, the issue of misinformation presents another challenge. Just as hashtags can unite people for a cause, they can also disseminate misguided beliefs or promote climate change denial. This necessitates the proactive role of platforms themselves to aggressively counter such misinformation.

7.7. Moving Forward: Future of #ClimateChange

The future of '#ClimateChange' depends on strategic use, continued engagement, and persistent digital advocacy. Social media platforms must continue to evolve their features, specifically improving credibility management mechanisms.

Opportunities for integrating with other digital tools like machine learning can enhance sentiment analysis, trend prediction, and effectiveness measurement. All these advancements, utilized prudently, can further fortify the position of hashtags in the global combat against climate change.

In summary, while hashtags represent a significant element of the climate struggle, they are just one piece of the puzzle. The action for a sustainable future calls for a multitude of efforts collectively, and being at the forefront of this struggle, the power and responsibility vested in digital tools like hashtags cannot be overstated. As pivotal tools, they should be leveraged responsibly and strategically for the successful orchestration of the digital-led, green revolution.

Chapter 8. Potential Pitfalls: The Challenges of Climate Action on Social Media

Diving into the chapter, we must first grasp the dynamic nature of the agile world of social media, which, although contributing prolifically to the spread of environmental information and manning the front lines of climate change consciousness, does not come without its own set of challenges. Indeed, as we attempt to weave the tangled web of climate change discourse through social media platforms, we stumble upon a number of multifaceted concerns, acting as inadvertent roadblocks in the otherwise smooth highway of digital activism.

8.1. The Muddy Waters of Misinformation

In the boundless world of the internet, misinformation and disinformation have become familiar terms. Unfortunately, content related to climate change isn't exempt from this. Climate change deniers often take to social platforms to spread misleading narratives or out-of-context information, muddying the mainstream comprehension of the urgency of the crisis. Furthermore, algorithms that prioritize sensationalist content can lead to the amplification of such damaging perspectives, while providing them a veneer of credibility.

Numerous studies demonstrate the mounting challenge posed by climate misinformation on social platforms. A worrisome finding in a 2020 report by The German Marshall Fund Digital New Deal project disclosed that climate disinformation content had engagement levels seven times higher than content from scientific sources. This onslaught of deceptive content not only hampers the general public's understanding of the issue, but it can also contribute to a psychological phenomenon known as "confirmation bias," where people seek out information that confirms their pre-existing beliefs and dismiss that which challenges them.

8.2. The Inequity of the Digital Divide

As we admire the democratization of information brought about by social media, we must also take into account the persistent issue of the digital divide – the gulf between those with ready access to digital technologies and the internet, and those who are yet to reap the benefits of this revolution.

While large sectors of the global population actively engage in climate change discourse on social platforms, a substantial number of people, particularly those from lower socio-economic backgrounds or less developed regions, might remain excluded. This not only slows the global spread of climate awareness, but also silences the voices of those most vulnerable to climate change in global conversations.

8.3. The Double-Edged Sword of Slacktivism

Another challenge lies in the phenomenon referred to as 'slacktivism' - the growing trend of supporting causes through simple measures, such as liking and sharing posts, signing e-petitions, or adding a supportive banner to one's profile picture. While these actions can indeed amplify a cause, they may sometimes give participants a false sense of accomplishment, reducing their motivation to engage in further, more impactful, actions. The ease and simplicity of online activism often mean that critical offline actions – such as reducing one's carbon footprint, voting for green policies, or participating in real-world demonstrations – may recede to the background, creating a disconnection between online fervor and tangible change.

8.4. An Echo Chamber of Opinions

Finally, a subtle but profound challenge appearing on the horizon is the formation of virtual echo chambers. An echo chamber is a digital environment where a person's beliefs are amplified or reinforced by communicating inside a closed system and repeated exposure to the same ideas. Instead of encouraging a exchange of diverse viewpoints and healthy debate, this one-sided flow of information can strengthen pre-existing biases and stifle critical thinking.

In conclusion, while the Internet's democratization and social media's reach have indeed broadened the spectrum of climate change conversation, navigating through the potential pitfalls remains crucial for collective climate action. Untangling the web of misinformation, addressing the digital inequity, encouraging meaningful participation beyond slacktivism, and breaking echo chambers should be integral parts of our digital climate strategies. As we continue to leverage these powerful communication tools, understanding these challenges is of the essence. It's the digital era's quest to ensure a sustainable future for generations to come—an ambition every bit as ambitious as putting a man on the moon. With cooperative, global efforts, and a digital world that is aware, tolerant, and motivated for action, this mammoth challenge may still prove surmountable.

Chapter 9. Influencers and Celebrities: Amplifying the Green Message

In today's world of snap decisions and fleeting attention spans, the influence that high-status individuals such as celebrities wield is indispensable. They have the power to command our attention and shape our perceptions, opinions, and actions. In the context of climate change, these societal trendsetters are using their platforms to disseminate the message of environmental awareness and sustainability.

9.1. The Relevance of Celebrities and Influencers in Today's Digital Society

It is a known fact that popular figures, celebrities and influencers alike, command significant audiences on social media. Given their broad fan bases, these influencers have the potential to affect change on a large scale. Many celebrities have taken on the mantle of environmental activism, using their notoriety to make this pressing issue more visible.

Social media powerhouse Kim Kardashian West, for instance, has used her reach to raise awareness about the California wildfires, a natural disaster exacerbated by global warming. Similarly, teen climate activist Greta Thunberg shot to international prominence through a single tweet, and now utilizes various online platforms to rally support for urgent climate action.

9.2. The Effective Use of Celebrity Power for Environmental Causes

Celebrities are effectively utilizing their reputation to encourage positive change on major environmental issues. From featuring in eye-opening documentaries to harnessing the reach of their music to send strong messages about climate change, there is no shortage of ways they are taking on climate change.

For example, in his documentary, "Before the Flood," actor and environmental activist Leonardo DiCaprio explored the harsh realities of climate change, drawing attention to the urgent need to react to this global crisis. Similarly, musician and activist Billie Eilish used her song, "All Good Girls Go To Hell," to visually represent the impacts of global warming and environmental destruction.

9.3. The Role of Influencers in Disseminating the Climate Change Message

Micro-influencers, or influencers with smaller but highly engaged audiences, also play significant roles in the fight against climate change. Many of them are using their online reach to promote sustainable practices, eco-friendly products and advocate for more significant action against climate change.

Travel influencers, for instance, are highlighting responsible tourism by sharing images of usually unseen pollution or suggesting sustainable alternatives. Health and lifestyle influencers, like Madeleine Olivia, provide tips on minimalistic living and plant-based diets as a way to lessen individual carbon footprints. These influencers have a knack for making climate action accessible and achievable for their followers, broadening the circle of individuals who are invested in ecological preservation.

9.4. The Potential Pitfalls: False Information and Performative Activism

While the involvement of influencers and celebrities in climate advocacy has mostly been positive, there are potential pitfalls. These include the spreading of misinformation, and performative activism – where influencers feign concern for climate change without actively or genuinely advocating for improvements in behavior or policy.

Misinformation may stem from a lack of thorough understanding of the complex issue of climate change. This makes it crucial for influencers and celebrities to base their advocacy on solid science and verified facts. Performative activism, on the other hand, can be counterproductive by fostering cynicism and eroding trust in climate action. It is therefore essential that influencers' and celebrities' climate advocacy is genuine and leads to actionable change, whether personal or at a policy level.

9.5. Concluding Thoughts: A Call to Responsible Influence

In conclusion, there is immense power in using popularity for good, especially in today's digital age. Influencers and celebrities who choose to amplify the green message are serving as catalysts for change by raising awareness and encouraging action on climate change. However, with great power comes even greater responsibility. These influential individuals need to ensure that they spread accurate information and advocate for genuine, actionable change. By doing so, they can inspire their followers to take important steps towards climate action, transforming their roles from mere trendsetters to changemakers in the battle against climate change.

Chapter 10. From Awareness to Action: Implementing Digital Strategies for Change

In an era surrounded by dazzling screens and beeping notifications, the pressing reality of climate change has found a unique avenue to enthrall and educate the masses. On this incredible online platform where posts meet passion, awareness about our planet's deteriorating health is transforming into action. This chapter will scrutinize the dynamic process of turning climate change cognizance into real-world efforts through efficient application of digital strategies.

10.1. Harnessing the Power of Social Media

Social media possesses a power that's as captivating as it is influential. Its ubiquitous presence and astounding potential reach around the globe fuel its potential as a formidable tool for environmental advocacy. But harnessing this power demands strategic utilization and optimized coordination of the platform's myriad features.

Developing digital strategies for climate change intervention begins with understanding social media platforms and their distinct characteristics. Facebook, with its detailed target demographic feature, allows advocacy groups to reach specific audiences effectively. Instagram's visually appealing format is excellent at fostering empathetic connections through impactful imagery, while Twitter's rapid, real-time information sharing capability makes it an ideal platform for real-time updates and mobilization.

10.2. Interactive Communication: A Key Strategy

Besides, throwing light on climate issues, effective digital strategies also require fostering interactive communication spaces. These platforms shouldn't merely act as bulletin boards; instead, they need to evolve into forums for discussions, debates, and exchange of ideas.

This bidirectional communication not only strengthens the community of climate advocates but also encourages naysayers to join the dialogue by creating a safe space for curiosity, questions, and debates. To this end, regularly hosting Q&A sessions, live chats with experts, and 'climate clubs' to discuss latest research findings can be instrumental.

10.3. Spotlights and Stories: The New Digital Storytelling

Social media offers a unique narrative style — Stories. This digital strategy breathes new life into environmental advocacy by adding a personal touch to abstract climate issues. By spotlighting real people impacted by climate change, organisations can create compelling stories that stimulate empathy and solidarity amongst users.

Similarly, campaigns that encourage individuals to share their climate actions can create a ripple effect of motivation, as every user feels seen, recognized and part of the broader climate change narrative. This seems trivial in front of the massive problem climate change presents, but these small actions together can yield impressive results at a global scale.

10.4. Taking Actions Beyond Likes and Shares

Creating awareness is a monumental initial step, but it's just that — an initial step. Social media platforms must help translate this newfound awareness into tangible actions. Sharing posts and clicking 'like' without any ensuing action can lead to what's known as 'slacktivism,' where users feel they've done their part simply by engaging virtually with an issue.

To combat this, digital strategies should incorporate calls-to-action (CTAs) in posts, urging users to donate, sign petitions, join local climate action groups, or make lifestyle changes. Information about actionable steps needs to be readily available, comprehensive, and easy to execute.

10.5. Usage of Analytics for Measuring Impact

Once digital strategies are in motion, analytics and metrics can offer insights into the effectiveness of the campaigns. Tools like Google Analytics, Facebook Insights, and Instagram Analytics can track engagement rates, audience demographics, post effectiveness, and more. This data can shape future strategies, making them more targeted, impactful, and results-driven.

In conclusion, the transformative journey from climate-change awareness to action involves strategizing, execution, and consistent evaluation. If implemented effectively, these digital strategies can harness the unparalleled potency of social media, mobilize global communities, and turn fleeting online engagements into substantial real-world actions. As we traverse this digital era, it is up to us to viscerally tap into the symbiotic relationship between social media and climate action. One post, one share, one story at a time, our combined efforts can indeed invite a much-needed change - a change that's not merely trending online but occurring in the real world.

Chapter 11. The Future of Social Media in Climate Change Advocacy

In an age where technology and digital platforms are weaving themselves into the very fabric of our society and culture, we cannot help but recognize the inherently transformative capacity of social media to advocate for central issues of our time, such as climate change. The dialogues and discourses taking place online echo the urgency of the current environmental crisis, penetrating deeper into the collective consciousness and influencing the behavior and actions of millions.

11.1. The Burgeoning Role of Social Media

Social media is no longer just a platform for interaction and connection. Today, it has emerged as a powerful tool, a change-maker, influencing public opinion and fueling global movements. In the context of climate change, social media platforms are becoming an instrumental advocate, aiding in the raising of awareness about current and future environmental challenges among diverse and disparate groups globally.

Platforms such as Twitter, Instagram, Facebook, and LinkedIn provide users with a digital stage from which they can voice their concerns, share information, and mobilize collective action. They have democratized access to climate change information, enabling users to bypass traditional gatekeepers and sources of information, connecting them directly with scientists, researchers, and leaders in the field. Due to this, social media enables not just a wider spread of information, but also sparks engagement. Users are prone to encounter differing viewpoints, engage in debates, and hone their understanding and perspectives on the critical issue of climate change.

11.2. e-Petitions and Crowd Funding: Facilitation of Grassroots Movements

Social media also brings new possibilities to life, such as initiating digital campaigns (e-petitions), driving fundraising efforts for environmental causes, and enabling ordinary people to play an extraordinary role in combating climate change. Through crowdfunding platforms that are often shared and publicized via social media, initiatives focused on climate change mitigation – from reforestation projects to renewable energy endeavors – are acquiring much-needed funding.

This democratic approach to funding makes each contributor feel like they're part of the solution, while e-petitions garner international signatures with ease, putting pressure on policymakers and corporations to prioritize environmental action. These online signatures represent a collective call to action, demonstrating how a digital platform can achieve real-world impact.

11.3. Social Media as an Arena for Climate Change Debates

Social media platforms are vibrant arenas where discussion, discourse, and debates on climate change are held. Global climate conversations happening on such platforms are essential to carving out powerful narratives that can resonate with billions. This helps in continually refining and contextualizing the global mission to combat climate change within the local context of millions of users.

Additionally, virtual debates help in addressing climate change skepticism and denial. With communicative and democratic exchanges, falsehoods can be challenged and facts can be brought to light. This interaction ultimately fosters an environment conducive to educational opportunities, helping to ensure that the general public is informed and aware of the realities of climate change.

11.4. Influence of Social Media Algorithms on Climate Advocacy

The pervasive penetration of social media is largely steered by underlying algorithms. These computational processes curate and customize the content served to each user, wholly shaping their digital experience. As much as they can be criticized for creating 'echo chambers' by promoting similar content, they also hold the potential to put climate change-related posts, digital activism, petitions, or crowdfunding initiatives on users' feeds. By understanding and leveraging these algorithms, climate change advocates can boost their reach, engagement, and influence on social media.

11.5. Integrating AI and Data Analytics: An Emerging Trend

Emerging technologies like Artificial Intelligence (AI) and big data analytics have begun to penetrate the domain of climate change advocacy on social media. These advanced tools provide an unparalleled ability to identify user trends, gauge public sentiment on climate-related matters, and streamline advocacy messages to resonate with different demographics. Implementing these technologies could potentially enhance the impact and influence of climate advocacy in the digital sphere.

11.6. Moving Forward: Uniting Digital Strategies with Real-world Action

As we navigate into a future fraught with environmental uncertainties, the cruciality of social media in climate advocacy rises. To ensure its effectiveness, digital strategies must be translated into offline, real-world actions. It's not enough for users to merely 'like', 'share,' or 'retweet'; they must feel compelled to change their behaviors, sign a petition, attend a protest, or donate to a cause.

In conclusion, the future of social media in climate change advocacy is not stagnant; it is evolving, persistently rearranging itself, seeking to optimize its transformative potential. As we strive towards a greener future, the digital revolution may be our most potent ally, but only if we recognize and harness its capacity effectively. The challenge lies in leveraging this global platform to spur international change – pushing us all toward a more sustainable path. As we ponder on the future of social media and environmental advocacy, one thing is clear. This digital revolution could very well be our generation's defining contribution towards combating climate change.

www.ingramcontent.com/pod-product-compliance
Lightning Source LLC
Chambersburg PA
CBHW071038260726
48661CB00007B/3050